ḤADĪTH
STATUS AND ROLE

An Introduction to the Prophet's Tradition

Sayyed Abul al-Ḥasan ʿAlī Ḥasanī Nadwī

UK ISLAMIC ACADEMY

ISBN 1 872531 75 X (PB)

Translated and Edited by Adil Salahi

General Editor: Iqbal Ahmad Azami

Published by

UK Islamic Academy
147 Mere Road, Highfields,
Leicester, LE5 5GQ
United Kingdom

Website: www.ukiabooks.com
E-mail: info@ukiabooks.com

British Library Cataloguing in Publication Data

A catalogue record for this book is available from the British Library

Design and Typeset by Muhammad al-Madani

بسم الله الرحمن الرحيم

CONTENTS

II: Ḥadīth and the Promotion of Islamic Climate and Attitudes

بسم الله الرحمن الرحيم

In the name of Allah, Most Gracious, Most Merciful

Introduction

Ḥadīth and the Shaping of Islamic Life

Perhaps no discipline has been subject to such attack over the entire period of Islamic history as has Ḥadīth. Attacks have been mounted from every quarter; some openly hostile, others subtle; some assuming an academic guise, others pretending to give due importance to the Qur'an. The fact is that since the early divisions within the Muslim community, leading to momentous changes in the leadership and the way the Muslim state was run, the Prophet's statements and traditions became a free-for-all, frequently raided by people who had no love for Islam or the Muslim community. Several groups of widely differing interests fabricated statements which they attributed to the Prophet, hoping to win support for their own political ambitions or deviant ideas. Some even came up with fabricated statements encouraging people to be stronger in faith and more diligent in worship. When reproached for their action and reminded of the authentic ḥadīth sternly warning anyone who knowingly attributes a falsehood to the Prophet, they absurdly retorted: "We are fabricating statements *for* him, not *against* him."

Since ḥadīth fabrication was rife during the period of splits and divisions, scholars of the highest calibre rose to the task of verification and authentication of *aḥādīth*. Their efforts produced fine results, developing the Ḥadīth corpus, a highly scholarly discipline that is unique to Islam and the Muslim community. No other nation or civilization has anything approaching such a thorough and meticulous methodology to verify the heritage of its founders. This has helped Muslims throughout history in following and practising their faith. It is particularly important to remember that many Islamic practices, including the main types of worship, such as prayer, zakat [i.e. obligatory charity] and pilgrimage, cannot be correctly offered or practised without reference to the Prophet's *aḥādīth* for guidance.

In more recent history, attacks against the Ḥadīth became more frequent, particularly since the second half of the nineteenth century. A number of Orientalists tried hard to discount the importance of the discipline. Goldziher and Schacht even questioned the most fundamental element in Ḥadīth study, namely, its reporting. With Orientalism adopting a general stand that is less outwardly critical of Islam, such attempts are given a distinctly academic tone. Nevertheless, they could not stand up to careful examination, and were shown by Muslim scholars to be basically flawed.

Other attacks on Ḥadīth in the twentieth century came from people who, as Muslims, professed to have the best interests of Islam at heart. There were several such attempts, some with political backing. They all tried to undervalue the importance of the Ḥadīth, claiming that Muslims would do much better if they would only rely on the Qur'an. Such people struggled hard to show that Islam can be followed and practised in total disregard of the Ḥadīth. All such attempts have come to nothing. How could they do otherwise, when the importance of following the Prophet's example is embodied in the first article of the Islamic faith, and expressed in the very declaration required of everyone who wants to be a Muslim. When we declare our belief that 'there is no deity other than God, and that Muhammad is God's Messenger,' we actually pledge to follow the Prophet in whatever he tells us as part of God's message. To argue that it is not incumbent on Muslims to follow the Prophet's Sunnah, which is embodied in the Ḥadīth, is to undermine Islam altogether by making the second part of the declaration devoid of substance.

Contemporary Muslim scholars have shown how hollow such arguments are. They have explained that without the Sunnah, no one can properly follow the Qur'an. They demonstrated the truth of a statement by earlier scholars who said: 'The Qur'an needs the Sunnah, more than the Sunnah needs the Qur'an.' This is perfectly true, because it is through the Sunnah that we learn how to implement the Qur'an.

It is by the grace of God that we have today a number of thorough scholarly studies defending the Sunnah as the second indispensable source of Islamic legislation. Besides, we have nothing to worry about with regard to the authenticity and reliability of the Sunnah. Attacks will continue to be voiced by suspect writers and aspirants to fame. But these will always meet the same fate as earlier ones: they will be short-lived whilst the Sunnah will remain a shining source showing Muslim individuals and communities how to conduct their lives in order to enjoy happiness both in this present life and in the life to come.

The present book includes two pamphlets on Ḥadīth, written in fine literary Arabic. The first introduces the Ḥadīth discipline and its development in the early period of Islamic history, up to the production of the six famous anthologies known as the Six Authentic Collections, or *al-Ṣiḥāḥ al-Sittah*. The other pamphlet tackles the role of Ḥadīth in shaping the social climate in Muslim societies. Together, the two explain the need for Ḥadīth in any Muslim community, and the reliability of its sources. As such, they are useful to most readers, including those who are well versed in the discipline. Abul-Hasan Nadwi shows that without Ḥadīth, no Muslim community can have the sort of social environment that Islam always produces. It has been my personal privilege to undertake the translation of these pamphlets.

London
Rajab 1426 A.H.
August 2005.

Adil Salahi

I

An Introduction to the Study of Ḥadīth

بسم الله الرحمن الرحيم

In the name of Allah, Most Gracious, Most Merciful

DIVINE WISDOM REFLECTED BY ḤADĪTH SCIENCES

The study of Ḥadīth is a science to which God guided the Muslim community in its early periods to pay much attention to. Thus the Muslim community has worked hard to preserve, document, and disseminate it, as well as to collect, check and ensure the accuracy of every ḥadīth attributed to the Prophet ﷺ. Indeed it has given much attention to every discipline and branch of study related to Ḥadīth. This clear guidance reflects God's wisdom and the special care He attached to the preservation and perfection of the Islamic faith. It has given the Muslim community an inborn and powerful motivation that it cannot suppress or overlook. It works like an effective drive, which is apparently too powerful to resist, but inherently too gentle to constitute any burden. On the contrary, the Muslim community derives much pleasure and inspiring gratification from responding to this powerful motivation. Hence, efforts have always been exerted, difficulties removed, and journeys undertaken in order to seek and collect *aḥādīth* from their reporters and transmitters. Great care has been taken to ensure the accurate reporting and transmission of *aḥādīth* from one locality to another. To this end, countless scholars, endowed with great intelligence and scholarship, dedicated themselves. Indeed no other community or civilization in the history of mankind can demonstrate similar care given to a discipline or branch of study.

As Prophethood is Sealed

All that we have said reflects God's definite purpose. It proves the great care God has attached to Prophet Muhammad's message, which is the final message He has sent to mankind, outlining the law that He has laid down for human life in all generations and communities to the end of time. It was His guidance that spurred the Muslim community to undertake different types of study at different times, as was necessary for a clear understanding of His message. Thus, we find the Muslim community paying much attention, at different times, to the preservation of the Ḥadīth, and to the deduction of rulings and their detailed application; to the pursuit of sciences derived from the Qur'an, such as linguistics, word-derivation and stylistics; to the production of dictionaries and the establishment of schools to teach the Qur'an and the Sunnah, as also paying special attention to character refinement, morality and self purification; to addressing the essence of faith and achieving a special degree of excellence in faith; and to paying careful consideration to the Prophet's guidance for the well being of heart and soul. These and other aspects of the guidance God has given to a long line of scholars, who combined a refined degree of faith and piety with in-depth knowledge and dedicated pursuit of learning, provide very clear evidence that, with Muhammad's message which He has perfected, God has brought the line of prophethood to its conclusion. It also indicates that divine care and preservation of Islam, as well as His support of its advocates, will never fail.

Better than Statues and Legends

Prophet Muhammad ﷺ occupies a unique position among all God's messengers and great men in history. He is the one about whom our knowledge covers all aspects of life, including his habits, manners, inclinations and desires, as well as his words and deeds, in detail and to an extent that is unmatched by our knowledge of anyone who died recently, or even of those who are our contemporaries. All this is due to the study of Ḥadīth which has documented for us his blessed life in all its details.

Old civilizations and followers of ancient religions used to draw images and paintings, or build statues of their prophets to represent them and to serve as reminders to contemporary and succeeding generations. This tradition gave birth to idolatry, as such statues came to be seen as idols and objects of worship. Different nations and communities continue to suffer from this legacy. God has been very kind to the Muslim community and to humanity at large when He prohibited the drawing of images of prophets and historical figures or the erecting of statues for anyone. He substituted all this by the Ḥadīth which provides a great number of speaking images that give us thorough knowledge of the Prophet ﷺ. We feel the happiness of his company as though we are with him, listening to his guidance, witnessing his actions and studying his life. For such a wealth of information to have been lost would have been a disaster of tragic proportions.

A Standard Measuring the Community's Worth

The Ḥadīth also provides an accurate barometer for reformers to evaluate the trends prevailing in their community so as to determine the extent of any deviation in the course it follows. An appropriate balance in morality, manners and actions can only be achieved through the Qur'an and the Ḥadīth combined. This is the only way to fill the vacuum that occurred when God's Messenger ﷺ passed away. Such a vacuum is part of God's law in this life.

وَمَا مُحَمَّدٌ إِلَّا رَسُولٌ قَدْ خَلَتْ مِن قَبْلِهِ ٱلرُّسُلُ ... ﴿١٤٤﴾

"*Muhammad is only a Messenger: all messengers have passed away before him...*" [Āl 'Imrān 3: 144].

إِنَّكَ مَيِّتٌ وَإِنَّهُم مَّيِّتُونَ ﴿٣٠﴾

"*You, [Muhammad,] are certainly bound to die, and they, too, are certainly bound to die.*" [Al-Zumar 39: 30].

The Ḥadīth provides an accurate representation of a perfectly balanced life. It outlines detailed directives by the Prophet ﷺ that are full of wisdom, and rulings that the Prophet ﷺ applied to Islamic society. Without these, the Muslim community would have erred so as to either indulge in excess or be complacent. Thus, imbalance would have prevailed. Furthermore, we would have lost the practical example God has required us to follow:

لَّقَدْ كَانَ لَكُمْ فِى رَسُولِ ٱللَّهِ أُسْوَةٌ حَسَنَةٌ ... ﴿٢١﴾

"*In God's Messenger you certainly have a good example to follow...*" [Al-Aḥzāb 33: 21].

قُلْ إِن كُنتُمْ تُحِبُّونَ ٱللَّهَ فَٱتَّبِعُونِى يُحْبِبْكُمُ ٱللَّهُ وَيَغْفِرْ لَكُمْ ذُنُوبَكُمْ ۗ
وَٱللَّهُ غَفُورٌ رَّحِيمٌ ﴿٣١﴾

"*Say: If you love God, follow me; God will love you and forgive you your sins.*" [Āl 'Imrān 3: 31].

Indeed it is from the Prophet's example that we derive confidence and strength, as well as reassurance that the implementation of Islam in life is both easy and practical.

Strong Motive for Reform and Resisting Deviation

The Prophet's Ḥadīth, which is a name that covers his verbal statements and practical guidance in general, is full of life, at once both powerful and persuasive. It has always strengthened people's motives to follow the Prophet's guidance and enhanced their God-fearing sense. It continues to motivate people to resist corruption and deviation from the right path. The Ḥadīth has indeed been the prime factor in the rise of many a reformer calling for emancipation that eliminates unwarranted practices, superstition and un-Islamic traditions, and advocating a full return to Islam in its pure and original version. Hence, for the Muslim community, the Ḥadīth is essential. It must be collected, documented and disseminated.

Delayed Documentation in the First Generation

Although a few of the Prophet's companions wrote down the *aḥadīth* and had their own collections,[1] many of them, particularly ʿUmar ibn al-Khaṭṭāb ﷺ, were highly reluctant to do so. ʿUmar ﷺ was very wise, and endowed with exceptional foresight in whatever related to the interests of Islam and Muslims as well as to the future of the Islamic religion. He, and others among the Prophet's companions, preferred to allow some time to pass before paying attention to the writing down and circulation of *aḥadīth*. Dr Muṣṭafā al-Sibāʿī, an eminent contemporary specialist in Ḥadīth, rightly says:

> Added to this was ʿUmar's desire that they should not frequently quote the Prophet's ḥadīth so that people

[1] Al-Sibāʿī, Muṣṭafā, *Al-Sunnah wa Makānatuhā fi al-Tashrīʿ al-Islamī*, Damascus, pp. 58-66.

> were not be preoccupied with ḥadīth in preference to the Qur'an.[2] At the time, the Qur'an was still a new revelation which the Muslims needed to study, memorize and make sure of its meanings. Al-Sha'bī quotes the following report by Quraẓah ibn Ka'b: "We set out on a journey to Iraq. 'Umar went with us to Ṣirār. He then stopped, did his ablutions and offered a two-*rak'ah* prayer before saying to us: 'Do you know why I have walked this far with you?' We said: 'Yes. We are the Prophet's companions and you liked to walk with us.' He said: 'You will come upon people who recite the Qur'an frequently, making a noise similar to the buzzing of bees. Do not give them the ḥadīth to divert their attentions. Pay more attention to the Qur'an and make only infrequent quotations from God's Messenger ﷺ. Set forth and I am your partner.' When Quraẓah arrived in Iraq, people asked him to tell them something of the Ḥadīth, but he refused, saying, ''Umar has ordered us not to do so.'"[3]

'Urwah ibn al-Zubayr (may God have mercy on him) reports that 'Umar ؓ intended to write down the ḥadīth,

---

[2] As happened in earlier religions and communities, when divine revelations became inextricably mixed with statements by prophets, scholars, and commentaries on scriptures, etc. The best example is the Jews' attitude to the Torah and the Talmud. It is often the case that the Talmud is more revered and relied upon than the Torah. Indeed the Jews often recite and study the Talmud, which contains the verbal laws and other Jewish traditions, more extensively than the Torah. The Talmud, which is often found in 12 volumes, contains commentaries, footnotes and quotes from rabbis and other Jewish figures.

[3] Al-Sibā'ī, op.cit. p. 63, quoting Ibn 'Abd al-Barr, *Jāmi' Bayān al-'Ilm*. Vol.2, p. 120.

and he consulted the Prophet's companions. They all suggested that he should do so. However, he waited for a month, seeking God's guidance. One morning he felt he had received such guidance. He said to the people:

> "I intended to write the Prophet's Sunnah, but I remembered a community before you who wrote books and became preoccupied with studying them, abandoning God's book. By God, I am not going to let anything be mixed with God's book."[4]

Ḥadīth Collection and Documentation

This task, most important as it was for the legislative, practical and scholarly future of the Muslim community, was, by God's will, destined to be undertaken by the later Caliph, ʿUmar ibn ʿAbd al-ʿAzīz, who was none other than ʿUmar ibn al-Khaṭṭāb's own grandson. Indeed, the first task he addressed after taking over as Caliph was the collection and preservation of *aḥādīth*. In doing so, he demonstrated his far-sightedness and sharp intelligence. Thus, he emulated his maternal grandfather, ʿUmar ibn al-Khaṭṭāb ﵁, who had earlier advised and urged Abū-Bakr ﵁, the first Caliph, to collect the Qur'an into one standardized version. By ʿUmar ibn ʿAbd al-ʿAzīz's time, there was no longer any fear that the *aḥādīth* might be mixed up or confused with the Qur'an. The number of people who knew the Qur'an by heart and the number of scholars who devoted themselves to the Qur'an in all areas of the Muslim world were too great to allow such confusion. This was in full realization of what God had stated and promised:

---

[4] Ibn ʿAbd al-Barr, *Jāmiʿ Bayān al-ʿIlm.* Vol.1 p. 76.

إِنَّا نَحْنُ نَزَّلْنَا ٱلذِّكْرَ وَإِنَّا لَهُۥ لَحَٰفِظُونَ ۝٩

> "*It is We who have revealed this Reminder; and it is We who will preserve it.*" [Al-Ḥijr 15: 9].

ʿUmar ibn ʿAbd al-ʿAzīz wrote to Abū Bakr ibn Muhammad ibn ʿAmr ibn Ḥazm, the Governor of Madinah, who was a scholar in his own right:

> "Collect what you can of the *aḥādīth* of God's Messenger and write them down; for I fear that knowledge may be lost and scholars may dwindle."

He also directed him to pay particular attention to the two collections of Ḥadīth belonging to ʿAmrah bint ʿAbd al-Raḥmān, a female Anṣārī scholar, and Qāsim ibn Muhammad ibn Abū Bakr, both of whom had devoted special attention to *aḥādīth*.

The effort ʿUmar ibn ʿAbd al-ʿAzīz started was not confined to Madinah and its governor. He wrote to the governors of all provinces instructing them:

> "Collect what you can of the *aḥādīth* of God's Messenger."[5]

Nor did ʿUmar ibn ʿAbd al-ʿAzīz limit his efforts to just urging scholars and governors to undertake this task. He took further measures to facilitate it, including allocating salaries for scholars, so that they could devote all their time to this pursuit without having to attend to earning their living by other means. Muhammad ibn ʿAbd al-Ḥakam reports:

---

[5] Abū Nuʿaym al-Aṣbahānī, *Tārīkh Aṣbahān*.

> ʿUmar ibn ʿAbd al-ʿAzīz sent Yazīd ibn Mālik and al-Ḥārith ibn Muhammad to the desert areas to teach the Sunnah to people, and he approved salaries for both of them. Yazīd accepted the salary but al-Ḥārith refused, saying: 'I would not accept a salary for disseminating what God has taught me.' When this was reported to ʿUmar ibn ʿAbd al-ʿAzīz, he said: 'To the best of my knowledge, there is no harm in what Yazīd has done, but may God give our community many more like al-Ḥārith.'[6]

Early Collection and Documentation

What took place during the short reign of ʿUmar ibn ʿAbd al-ʿAzīz, with regard to collecting the Ḥadīth and committing it to writing, was not an unprecedented development. Interest in writing down the Ḥadīth started during the lifetime of the Prophet ﷺ and shortly after his death, but the process was neither official nor systematic. Works of history and biography mention a number of Ḥadīth collections attributed to the scholars who undertook the task of collecting and writing them. Hence, we know that ʿAbdullāh ibn ʿAmr ibn al-ʿĀṣ had his collection of Ḥadīth which he named al-Ṣādiqah,[7] ʿAlī ibn Abī Ṭālib رضي الله عنه had his *Ṣaḥīfah*,[8] while Anas had his own collection which he took with him when people gathered to listen to *aḥādīth*. Ḥadīth collection and writing was also reported to have been undertaken by ʿAbdullāh ibn ʿAbbās,[9] ʿAbdullāh ibn Masʿūd[10] and Jābir ibn ʿAbdullāh رضي الله عنهم.[11]

---

6 Ibn ʿAbd al-Ḥakam, *Sīrat ʿUmar ibn ʿAbd al-ʿAzīz*, p. 167

7 Ibn ʿAbd al-Barr, op.cit, Vol. 1, p. 72.

8 Al-Bukhārī, *Ṣaḥīḥ, Kitāb al-ʿIlm, Bāb Kitābat al-ʿIlm.*

9 Al-Tirmidhī, *al-ʿIlal.*

10 Ibn ʿAbd al-Barr, op.cit. , Vol. 1, p. 72.

11 Muslim, *Ṣaḥīḥ.*

Indeed, the *Ṣaḥīfah* written by Hammām ibn Munabbih (d. 101 or 102 AH), who was a student of Abū Hurayrah, the Prophet's companion, indicates a process of development in Ḥadīth documentation. For it was written as dictated by Abū Hurayrah, who died in 58 AH, to Hammām. This is indeed the oldest collection we have in full.[12]

By the middle of the second century, scholarship in collecting and documenting Ḥadīth gathered momentum. Its main figures during this century were Ibn Shihāb al-Zuhrī (d. 124 AH), Ibn Jurayj of Makkah (d. 150), Ibn Isḥāq (d. 151), Muʿammar of Yemen (d. 153), Saʿīd ibn ʿArūbah of Madinah (d. 156), al-Rabīʿ ibn Ṣubayḥ (d. 160), Sufyān al-Thawrī (d. 161), Mālik ibn Anas, the author of *al-Muwaṭṭa'*, (d. 179), al-Layth ibn Saʿd (d. 175), Ibn al-Mubārak (d. 181). Numerous other scholars followed in their footsteps.[13]

The Six Authentic Collections

Thus, Ḥadīth was the subject of much care and interest by the Muslim community, second only to the Qur'an.

---

[12] Hammām ibn Munabbih's *Ṣaḥīfah* was discovered in the manuscript departments of the libraries of al-Ẓāhiriyyah in Damascus, Berlin and the University of Ankara. It was then published in four instalments in the magazine of the Arabic Language Academy, *Majallat al-Majmaʿ al-ʿIlmī al-ʿArabī*, Damascus, 1953. It was later published separately with scholarly editing in a book entitled *Ṣaḥīfah Hammām ibn Munabbih*, by Dr Muhammad Ḥamīdullāh, Hayderabad, 1955. The book, published in Urdu, includes a list of the Ḥadīth scrolls and documents written during the Prophet's lifetime.

[13] For a detailed discussion of collecting and documenting Ḥadīth in the first two centuries of the Islamic calendar, please refer to M.M. Azami, *Studies in Hadith Methodology and Literature*, American Trust Publication, Indianapolis, 1977, and *Studies in Early Hadith Literature*, (the same publisher), 1978.

Scholars of high calibre and great integrity and achievement dedicated their efforts to its collection, documentation, and careful checking for maximum accuracy and authenticity. Their efforts were instrumental in collecting from the numerous sources scattered all over the Muslim world a number of accurate and verified anthologies of Ḥadīth. The most important of these are the six agreed by scholars of Islamic studies, and Ḥadīth in particular, to be ahead of the rest in accuracy and authenticity. These are *al-Jāmiʿ al-Ṣaḥīḥ* by al-Bukhārī, *al-Jāmiʿ al-Ṣaḥīḥ* by Muslim, *al-Jāmiʿ* by al-Tirmidhī, *al-Sunan* by Abū Dāwūd, *al-Sunan* by al-Nasāʾī, and *al-Sunan* by Ibn Mājah.[14] Scholars refer to them collectively as the Six Authentic Collections.

Among these six collections, two are even more distinguished than the rest, and widely more accepted and studied. These are *al-Jāmiʿ al-Ṣaḥīḥ* by Muhammad ibn Ismāʿīl ibn Ibrāhīm al-Juʿafī al-Bukhārī (d. 256), and *al-Jāmiʿ al-Ṣaḥīḥ* by Muslim ibn al-Hajjāj al-Qushayrī al-Naisāpūrī (d. 261). Together they are referred to as *al-Ṣaḥīḥān*, or the Two Authentic Ones. If a ḥadīth is related in both these two collections, it is said to be *muttafaq ʿalayh*, which means 'agreed upon'. This gives it an even higher degree of authenticity. In his book, *Ḥujjat Allah al-Bālighah*, the most authoritative Ḥadīth scholar in later generations, Shaykh Ahmad ibn ʿAbd al-Raḥīm al-Dehlawī (d. 1176 AH), states:

> "As for the two *Ṣaḥīḥ* collections, scholars of Ḥadīth are agreed that any ḥadīth they relate which has a continuous chain of transmission going up to the Prophet ﷺ and directly quoting him is certainly authentic. Scholars are also agreed that these two collections

[14] Imam Mālik's *al-Muwaṭṭaʾ* should be included with these. We will speak about this later.

> enjoy the grade of *mutawātir* up to the two scholars who collected and produced them. Anyone who belittles them is a deviant person who follows a line other than that followed by true believers."[15]

The six authentic collections continue to be an important resource for reform and sound Islamic thought in the Muslim community. Scholars and advocates of Islam continue to refer to them for a proper understanding of Islam and for clear thinking on its priorities. They base their efforts and arguments on the *aḥādīth* related in these collections, which form the basis of their advocacy of Islam in its true form and their campaigns against deviation and corruption. No one who wants his Muslim community to regain a pure Islamic image can do without these six collections. How else can he establish a relationship between his community and the life of the Prophet ﷺ whose example we are required to follow? Moreover, they are an indispensable resource for scholars who need to deduce rulings for contemporary situations.

---

[15] Al-Dehlawi, *Ḥujjat Allah al-Bālighah*, Vol. 1, p. 106.

BIOGRAPHICAL NOTES ON THE AUTHORS OF THE SIX AUTHENTIC COLLECTIONS

IMAM AL-BUKHĀRĪ,[16] AUTHOR OF *AL-JĀMIʿ AL-ṢAḤĪḤ*

Abū ʿAbdullāh, Imam Muhammad ibn Ismāʿl ibn Ibrāhīm ibn al-Mughīrah ibn Bardazbeh al-Juʿafī al-Bukhārī, the author of the *Ṣaḥīḥ* and other collections and classifications, was born in the month of Shawwāl 194 AH, corresponding to 810 CE. He lost his father in his childhood. After having learnt all the *aḥādīth* related in his hometown, he travelled with his mother and brother in 210 AH to Balkh, before going on to Makkah, Basrah and Kufah, where he studied under the leading scholars of these cities. He then travelled on to Syria where he attended the main scholars in ʿAsqalān, Damascus and Ḥumṣ. He started to teach Ḥadīth and to prepare collections and classifications of Ḥadīth at a young age, or 'before he had a single hair on his face,' as his biographers say. He was without peers in his intelligence, knowledge, worship and dedication. Among his large number of students who reported *aḥādīth* learnt from him was al-Tirmidhī. He is quoted as saying: "I have written down what I heard from more than 1000 men." Muhammad ibn Khamāraweih quotes him as saying: "I know by heart 100,000 authentic *aḥādīth* and 200,000 *aḥādīth* which are less

---

16 Our main source for all these biographical notes is *Tadhkirat al-Ḥuffāẓ*, by Imam Muhammad al-Dhahbī (d. 748)

than authentic." Ibn Khuzaymah says: "No one on the face of the earth has better knowledge of Ḥadīth than al-Bukhārī." He died on the night of ʿĪd al-Fiṭr in 256 AH.

A Test of Peers

There are many reports about the excellence of al-Bukhārī's scholarship and his fascinating memory. One of the most amazing reports mentions that on his arrival in Baghdad, a number of Ḥadīth scholars thought of putting him to a test in order to establish whether his reputation was deserved or not. After some deliberation, they came up with a plan, selecting 100 *aḥādīth*, and switching their texts and chains of transmission around, so that the text of each ḥadīth would have a chain of transmitters belonging to a different ḥadīth. They selected ten scholars, giving to each one ten of these *aḥādīth* that had been tampered with. They were supposed to put these patched up *aḥādīth* to al-Bukhārī in public. They arranged with him a time for a study circle in the main mosque which they all attended, including the ten scholars with the *aḥādīth* in question, and they invited a number of people so that the circle was well attended by both scholars and laymen.

When the circle was in progress, one of the ten scholars stood up and put to him the first of his ten tampered with *aḥādīth*, asking him how he graded it, but al-Bukhari said: 'I do not know this one.' He then put to him the remaining nine *aḥādīth*, but each time, al-Bukhārī gave the same answer: 'I do not know this one.' The scholars who were aware of what was going on whispered to one another: 'The man has discovered the game.' But ordinary people felt that al-Bukhārī was a very ordinary scholar. The other nine scholars did the same asking him about each one of their falsified *aḥādīth*, and each time he gave exactly the same answer, giving no further indication of his understanding. When all had finished, and he realized that there were no further questions, he looked at the first man and said: 'Your first question quoted the following, but this is incorrect and the correct ḥadīth is so and so. Then you asked me about the following and the correct version is such and such.' He put to him all the ten questions in the wrong way the man had delivered them, and gave to each the correct version. He then did the same with the other nine men, quoting each of his ten questions and then putting them into their correct versions, giving each text its correct chain of transmission and attaching each chain to its correct text. All people attending the mosque were unanimous that he was a scholar of the highest calibre.

Imam Ibn Ḥajar, who wrote a voluminous commentary on al-Bukhārī's *Ṣaḥīḥ* comments:

> "With al-Bukhārī's high scholarship, it is no wonder that he could put each ḥadīth correctly. What is most amazing is that he was able to repeat from memory all those wrong *aḥādīth*, in the order they were put to him, when he had only heard them once."

Distinctive Characteristics of al-Bukhārī's *Ṣaḥīḥ*

We do not know of any book of a religious nature, by a human being, which has been subject to as many comments, explanations and annotations by scholars in successive generations as has this book which is considered the second most accurate work after the Qur'an. In earlier periods, commentaries, interpretations and annotations were the methods which revealed the extent to which scholars cared about and were interested in a certain book. The more of these written about a particular book, the higher its rank among scholarly works and the greater its fame in academic circles. Conversely, books that received little such attention were unlikely to receive public interest. As this was the only criterion to assess the success of any work in earlier generations, we can decisively conclude that al-Bukhārī's *Ṣaḥīḥ* occupies prime position among Islamic works produced anywhere in the world at any time since the revelation of the Qur'an and the start of advocacy of the Islamic message up to the present day. No less than 131 books by way of commentary and annotation have been written about al-Bukhārī's authentic collection. The number may be even greater. This total is based only on a few indexes compiled by scholars, such as *Kashf al-Ẓunūn* by al-Ḥalabī, *Miftāḥ al-Saʿādah* by Ṭāsh Kubrā Zadeh, *Itḥāf al-Nubalā', al-Dībāj al-Mudhahhab, Nayl al-Ibtihāj,* and the introductions to various commentaries and annotations, as well as *al-Thaqāfah al-Islāmiyah fi al-Hind* by ʿAbd al-Ḥayy al-Ḥasanī, the former Director of Nadwat al-ʿUlamā' (d. 1341 AH) and some of his individual research efforts. There is no doubt that the Muslim world is far wider than geographers imagine and Islamic history extends much further than historians believe. There may be many a treasure hidden in a little corner.

Ibn Ḥajar's commentary known as *Fatḥ al-Bārī*, in 13 very large volumes and an extensive introduction, could be treated as a complete library in Ḥadīth disciplines. It is without equal in the history of any religious faith. The Muslim community should proudly introduce this great scholarly work to scholars and researchers in religion, philosophy and human civilization and culture. It provides clear evidence of the Muslim community's exceptional scholarly efforts and advancement, and the extra care it has always taken of the Prophet's heritage, studying it thoroughly and profoundly.

We do not in any way underestimate the value of other commentaries written on al-Bukhārī's *Ṣaḥīḥ*, particularly *ʿUmdat al-Qārī* by Badr al-Dīn al-ʿAynī in 11 volumes, constituting a complete library of linguistics and literary disciplines, as well as in the deduction of rulings and other conclusions.[17]

The second important criterion to judge a book is the time allocated to its study, and the keen interest in copying and disseminating it, as well as competing in learning or memorizing it. All this has continued, generation after generation, and by one class of scholars after another, to the extent that the *Ṣaḥīḥ* was never allowed to be out of keen academic and scholarly interest during any period of history. Such keen interest has preserved it free of any distortion or alteration. We can say without fear of contradiction that al-Bukhārī's *Ṣaḥīḥ* enjoys such distinction, ranking second only to God's book, the Qur'an. No less than 90,000 scholars and reporters received this book from its author in chains of transmission leading up to its compiler. It has attained the rank of *mutawātir*[18] in its popularity and accurate reporting up to its author. No one will deny this except one who doubts what is *mutawātir* or proven scientific fact. The book continues to receive much interest, study and research in scholarly institutions throughout the Muslim world.

---

[17] We may also add the commentary known as *Irshād al-Sārī* by al-Qasṭalānī, in 10 volumes.

[18] This describes a statement or a text reported by a number of scholars or reporters at every stage which is large enough to preclude any possibility of reporting something they know to be false: Editor's note.

Chapters and Notes of Special Importance

Scholars devoted to the study, teaching, classification and commentary on Ḥadīth are agreed that the chapter divisions, headings and notes made by al-Bukhārī are of the finest quality, reflecting his keen intelligence. Indeed, his notes and headings are a distinctive feature, giving his work a position of superiority among books of authentic *aḥādīth*, great as these may be. Furthermore, scholars are graded in their excellence, originality and insight on the basis of their understanding of this great book and their ability to unlock its treasures and uncover the author's purpose. No one is awarded a position of excellence in Ḥadīth scholarship or teaching, experienced in such matters as he may be, unless he has studied this work in depth and presented it with true clarity. Hence, scholars of both olden and recent times gave priority in their attention to this work and made it the subject of much of their work. Indeed, no literary critic has ever made an effort into explaining and interpreting even the finest poems, rich as they may be in images and figures of speech, which could approach, let alone exceed, the profound effort exerted by scholars who wrote commentaries on al-Bukhārī's *Ṣaḥīḥ*. No other work has received as much attention as al-Bukhārī's.

The great subtlety encountered in chapter headings and notes made by al-Bukhārī reflects his great variety of purpose and depth of understanding, as well as his exceptional intelligence. It also reflects a keen desire by the author to give maximum benefit to others. He may be likened to a bee keen to have its full capacity of fine pollen in order to make from it pure honey that is certain to cure illness.

Imam Muslim ibn al-Ḥajjāj al-Qushayrī

Abu al-Ḥusayn Muslim ibn al-Ḥajjāj al-Qushayrī al-Naisapūrī is said to have been born in 204 AH, and that he started his study of Ḥadīth in 218. Imām Aḥmad ibn Ḥanbal was among a large number of scholars from whom Muslim learnt the Ḥadīth. Many scholars have praised him highly, even during his own time. Aḥmad ibn Salamah says:

> 'I know that Abū Zarʿah and Abū Ḥātim put Muslim ibn al-Ḥajjāj ahead of the top scholars of their generation in his knowledge of authentic Ḥadīth.

Abū Quraysh is quoted as saying:

> 'The top scholars of Ḥadīth in the world are four. Muslim is one of them.'

Muhammad ibn al-Māsarjī reports that he heard Muslim saying:

> 'I have sorted out this authentic collection from three hundred thousand *aḥādīth* I have reported from other scholars.'

Ibn al-Sharqī quotes Muslim as saying:

> 'I have not included anything in this book of mine without solid proof and I have not omitted anything unless I have solid proof.'

Muslim died in the month of Rajab in 261 AH.

Like all great scholarly works produced by those who have a high level of expertise, commitment and dedication, and who study under the leaders in their field, Muslim's *Ṣaḥīḥ* has its own distinctive characteristics, the most important of which are:

1. It provides an easy reference tool. Muslim places each ḥadīth at its most suitable place where he includes all the versions and chains of transmission he has selected. Thus, students and scholars find it easier to look at all the different versions, highlighting the relevant points that appear through easy comparison. It is also far more reassuring as regards the reliability of a ḥadīth to look at all its authentic versions.

2. Moreover, Muslim includes the whole text of a ḥadīth, long as it may be, at the same place. He only rarely repeats a ḥadīth under different chapters or headings.

3. The *Ṣaḥīḥ* by Muslim has only a short prologue after which it addresses the task of reporting *aḥādīth*. It does not include anything else apart from highly authentic statements by selected people from the generation that succeeded the Prophet's companions, and the following generation, as well as some *Fiqh* texts. It makes no attempt to deduce rulings.

4. Muslim also takes care to point out differences of reporting, attributing any statement to its particular reporter. Thus, he may say, 'We have been told by X and Z, but the actual text reproduced here is the one by X, etc.' If the two reports differ in certain wordings in the text of the ḥadīth, or in identifying a certain reporter, Muslim takes care to mention these differences.

5. It is the second highest ranking book of Ḥadīth dedicated only to what is authentic. It is second only to al-Bukhārī's *Ṣaḥīḥ*.

Imām Abū Dāwūd al-Sijistānī

Sulaymān ibn al-Ashʿath ibn Isḥāq ibn Bashīr al-Azdī al-Sijistānī, who classified the *Sunan* anthology, was born in 202 AH. He studied Ḥadīth, listening to it being reported by a large number of scholars in Hijaz, Syria, Egypt, Iraq, Persia and other places. He is quoted by top scholars such as al-Tirmidhī, al-Nasā'ī and many others. His teacher, Aḥmad ibn Ḥanbal, relates a ḥadīth reported by him. Abū Dāwūd also showed him his own book for peer review and Aḥmad commended his work. Muhammad ibn Isḥāq al-Ṣāghātī says:

> 'The reporting of Ḥadīth was made easy for Abū Dāwūd just like work with iron was made easy for the Prophet David.'

Abū Dāwūd is quoted as saying:

> 'I have included in my book only what is authentic or very close to being authentic. If I include a ḥadīth that is clearly suspect, I make sure to point this out.'

Al-Ḥākim Abū ʿAbdullāh says:

> 'Abū Dāwūd was, without any doubt, the leading figure among Ḥadīth scholars in his own time.'

Abū Dāwūd died in Basrah on 16 Shawwāl 275 AH.

Abū Dāwūd's *Sunan* is one of the books of Ḥadīth which have received universal acceptance. It has been the subject of much care and attention by leading scholars of Ḥadīth, placing it among the top reference books throughout all periods of Islamic scholarly history. It is considered the third or fourth pillar supporting the elevated structure of the Sunnah. Shaykh al-Islam Yaḥyā ibn Sharaf al-Nawawī, who wrote a commentary on Muslim's *Ṣaḥīḥ*, says:

> 'Anyone who studies Ḥadīth, and indeed all people, should certainly study the *Sunan* by Abū Dāwūd and know it well. Most *aḥādīth* forming the basis of rulings are included in it. Coupled with this are its distinctive qualities of easy reference, and the expertise and attentive care of its author.

Imām Ibn al-Qayyim, the author of *Zād al-Maʿād* says:

> 'This book has become the final say in any dispute. It is the reference point for scholars of integrity and diligence. '

The book has received great attention by scholars who commented on it and annotated it. Perhaps one of its best and most useful commentaries is *Sharḥ Maʿālim al-Sunan* by Ḥamad ibn Muhammad ibn Ibrāhīm al-Khaṭṭābī (d. 388 AH). It includes many discussions of profound insight and useful detail.[19]

---

[19] One of the more recent commentaries on Abū Dāwūd's *Sunan* is *ʿAwn al-Maʿbūd* by Shams al-Ḥaq al-ʿAẓīm'ābādī. This commentary has been published many times, with recent editions in 14 volumes plus 2 volumes of indexes.

Imām al-Tirmidhī

Imām Abū ʿĪsā Muhammad ibn ʿĪsā ibn Sawrah al-Sulamī al-Tirmidhī, the author of *Al-Jāmiʿ* and *Al-ʿIlal*, studied Ḥadīth under Qutaybah ibn Saʿīd, Abū Musʿab, Ibrāhīm ibn ʿAbdullāh al-Harawī and many others. He acquired his fine scholarly sense of Ḥadīth from al-Bukhārī. In his book *Al-Thiqāt*, Ibn Ḥibbān says:

> 'Abū ʿĪsā was distinguished among scholars. He made collections, classified, learnt by heart and compared his learning with others.'

Al-Ḥākim quotes ʿUmar ibn ʿAlk as saying:

> 'When al-Bukhārī died, he left nobody in Persia who could excel Abū ʿĪsā in his knowledge, memory, piety and dedication.'

Among the numerous scholars who received the Ḥadīth from al-Tirmidhī was none other than al-Bukhārī. Al-Tirmidhī died in Tirmidh, or Termiz as it is often spelled, on 13 Rajab 279 AH.

Al-Tirmidhī is distinguished as being the first scholar ever to go into what we call today comparative *Fiqh*. We are greatly indebted to him for the preservation of the conclusions of the different schools of Islamic law in his generation. Without him, much of this would have been lost. This is the main distinctive quality of his book, *al-Jāmiʿ*, which is not shared by any other Ḥadīth anthology. It is one of the most reliable reference books and the oldest that tackles differences over legal issues. It is particularly important in giving the views of some schools that have not survived, such as those of al-Awzāʿī and al-Thawrī and

Isḥāq ibn Rāhaweih. One of its important features is the fact that it has preserved for later generations the views of Imām al-Shāfiʿī's old school.

Al-Tirmidhī's book, *al-Jāmiʿ*, is practically the main reference in identifying the *aḥādīth* of the *ḥasan* or 'acceptable' grade, which is a grade of authenticity that is a little lower than *ṣaḥīḥ* or authentic. This represents a wealth of invaluable information that cannot be overlooked. We do not know of any of the great scholars of Ḥadīth who has given this aspect similar attention. Imām Abū ʿAmr ibn al-Ṣalāḥ says:

> 'Al-Tirmidhī's book is definitive in knowing the *ḥasan aḥādīth*. It is he who has given it its name and gave it frequent mention.'[20]

Al-Tirmidhī paid particular attention to the study of reporters' reliability which constitutes the disciplines known as *ʿIlm al-Rijāl* and *ʿIlm al-Jarḥ wal-Taʿdīl*. The first studies the personal history of reporters and the second gives a rating of the reliability of each reporter, classifying him or her as reliable, acceptable, or rejected. Further classifications may be included under these headings. Certain aspects of the study of chains of transmission are the exclusive reserve of al-Tirmidhī, and these are only known to people of high achievement in Ḥadīth studies. The book has many other special features.

---

[20] Ibn al-Ṣalāḥ, *ʿUlūm al-ḥadīth,* pp. 14-15.

IMĀM IBN MĀJAH

Abū ʿAbdullāh Muhammad ibn Yazīd ibn Mājah al-Qazwīnī, who classified *Al-Sunan* anthology and authored other books on Qur'anic commentary and history, was born in 209 AH. He attended many of the great authorities on Ḥadīth of his age. Abū Yaʿlā al-Khalīlī says: 'Ibn Mājah is a reliable scholar of high standing who has earned wide approval. He is an authority on Ḥadīth. He travelled to Iraq and Iran as well as to Makkah, Syria and Egypt.' His *Sunan* includes some *aḥādīth* that are not at the same level of authenticity as those given in other collections of *Ṣaḥīḥ* and *Sunan*. Ibn Mājah died in 273 AH. Abū al-Ḥasan al-Qaṭṭān, a close associate of Ibn Mājah, says: '*Al-Sunan* includes no less than 1500 headings, but its mere total is not more than four thousand *aḥādīth*.

IMAM AL-NASĀ'Ī

Imām Aḥmad ibn Shuʿayb ibn ʿAlī ibn Sinān ibn Baḥr al-Nasā'ī of Khurāsān in Iran, a judge and author of *al-Sunan*, was born in 215 AH. He studied Ḥadīth listening to scholars such as Qutaybah ibn Saʿīd, Isḥāq ibn Rāhaweih, and Hishām ibn ʿAmmār and many others of their calibre in Iran, Iraq, Hijaz, Egypt, Syria and elsewhere. He excelled in this field and was recognized as a leading scholar, and a meticulous Ḥadīth expert who reported *aḥādīth* with short chains of transmission. He later settled in Egypt.

He authored, in Damascus, a book, *Al-Khaṣā'iṣ*, on ʿAlī's characteristics, because he realized that many people did not appreciate his importance, merit and high standing. He then wrote a book on the fine characters and characteristics of the Prophet's companions. His contemporary scholars describe at length his great devotion and his worship both during the night and the day. They also mention that he was in the Egyptian army on one of its campaigns. Al-Dāraquṭnī says that al-Nasā'ī died in 303 AH, but we have different reports concerning the place of his death. He is, however, buried in Makkah between al-Ṣafā and al-Marwah.

Imām Mālik

To complement these notes on the scholars who compiled the six authentic collections we need to add a note on Imām Mālik ibn Anas ibn Mālik, a scholar of the highest calibre and the founder of one of the four major schools of *Fiqh*, or Islamic law. He is the author of *Al-Muwaṭṭa'*, one of the most celebrated books in Ḥadīth scholarship. Chronologically, it comes before the six collections. Moreover, it led the way in various aspects of Ḥadīth scholarship, and has received universal acceptance. Nevertheless, the six authentic collections have received much care and attention, in scholarly and research circles. Hence, we had to introduce them ahead of *al-Muwaṭṭa'* and its highly respected author, the leading scholar of Madinah. If a scholar is introduced later than his peers, it does not follow that he is less in rank or esteem.[21]

Imām Mālik ibn Anas ibn Mālik, was a highly renowned and unanimously acclaimed scholar of *Fiqh* and Ḥadīth, the Imam of the Prophet's capital, Madinah. Al-Shāfiʿī says:

> 'When scholars are mentioned, Mālik is the star among them,'

and,

> 'All scholarship in Hijaz would have been lost, had it not been for Mālik and Sufyān ibn ʿUyaynah;'

and,

> 'No book of scholarship on the face of the earth is more correct and accurate than *al-Muwaṭṭa'*.'

---

[21] Some scholars consider *al-Muwaṭṭa'* as one of the six authentic collections, in place of Ibn Mājah's *al-Sunan*.

Wahīb says:

> 'Among scholars of ḥadīth, Mālik is the leading figure.'

His circle was characterized by seriousness and scholarship. He himself was held in awe, and he allowed no futile argument, idle talk, or loud voices. Strangers might ask him about a certain ḥadīth, and his answer would consist of relating one ḥadīth after another.

In his book, *Tadhkirat al-Ḥuffāẓ*, *al*-Dhahbī says: 'Mālik combined a number of qualities which, to my knowledge, no other scholar enjoyed:

1. a long life and learning from early scholars;
2. keen intelligence, a penetrative mind and broad knowledge;
3. common acceptance by scholars of his high standing and accurate reporting;
4. universal acknowledgement of his piety, integrity and commitment to the Prophet's Sunnah; and,
5. his leading position in *Fiqh*, legal rulings and sound basis'. He lived 86 years, as the most reliable report puts his birth in 93 and his death in 179 AH.

Mālik reported *aḥādīth* he heard directly from Nāfiʿ, al-Muqbirī, Naʿīm al-Mujammar, al-Zuhrī, ʿĀmir ibn ʿAbdullāh ibn al-Zubayr, Ibn al-Munkadir, ʿAbdullāh ibn Dīnār and many others. A countless number of Ḥadīth transmitters reported what they heard from him. His school of *Fiqh*, or Islamic law, is followed in North Africa, from Sudan to Morocco, and was followed in the Andalus.

His book, *Al-Muwaṭṭa'*, in two different versions is reported by two of Mālik's most distinguished students. The first is that reported by Yaḥyā al-Laythī al-Maṣmūdī of the Andalus. It is this version that comes immediately to mind whenever the book is mentioned. This has received great care and attention by scholars in the past and in recent days. The other version is that reported by Imām Muhammad ibn al-Ḥasan al-Shaybānī, Imam Abū Ḥanīfah's disciple. Some Ḥadīth experts give this latter version preference over the first for a variety of reasons.[22]*

One of the latest commentaries on this priceless book is *Awjaz al-Masālik ilā Muwaṭṭa' Mālik* by the renowned Ḥadīth scholar Muhammad Zakariyā al-Kandahlawī. It is published with two introductions, one by the present author and the other by Muhammad Yusuf al-Bannūrī, a scholar of high standing. This commentary provides a wealth of knowledge, is rich in material, and puts together much valuable information that is scattered across numerous books on a wide variety of subjects. It can be aptly described as a mini-encyclopaedia on *Al-Muwaṭṭa'* and its great author. It

---

22 The renowned scholar ʿAbd al-Hayy ibn ʿAbd al-Halim al-Ansaari of Lucknow (d. 1304 AH) published a commentary on this version which is full of useful information and valuable comparisons, entitled *Al-Taʿliq al-Mumajjad ʿala Muwatta' Muhammad*. The book has been edited by Dr Taqiy al-Din Nadwi, and published in three volumes in Damascus with two introductions, one by the present author and the other by Shaykh ʿAbd al-Fattah Abu Ghuddah. It is an invaluable book for students and scholars.

* Scholars differ in their views on which version is better. In fact, as Shaykh Muhammad Abu Zahrah, a leading scholar of the 20th century mentions in his book on Imam Malik, "the difference between the two versions is not extensive, which confirms that they have the same origin, and their attribution to Malik is undoubtedly correct." Muhammad ibn al-Hasan's version has a smaller number of *aḥadīth* in certain chapters. Most scholars prefer Yahya's version. Perhaps those who prefer the other version take into account that its reporter, Muhammad ibn al-Hasan, mentions his own views on questions in which he differs with Malik, just like he does with his own teacher, Abu Hanifah. – Editor's note.

also provides much useful information about India and Indian scholars of Ḥadīth, including the author's teachers, as well as many essential principles, concepts and valuable hints and tips.

OTHER ḤADĪTH COLLECTIONS

There are numerous other Ḥadīth collections which have received wide acceptance, proving to be of great help to scholars in consolidating the foundation of their views and schools of law. These include *Al-Āthār* by Imām Abū Ḥanīfah, *Al-Musnad* by Imām Aḥmad ibn Ḥanbal, *Al-Musnad* by Abū Dāwūd al-Ṭayālisī, *Sharḥ Maʿānī al-Āthār* by al-Ṭaḥāwī, the three *Muʿjam*s by Imam Sulaymān ibn Aḥmad al-Ṭabarānī, *Al-Sunan* by al-Dāraquṭnī, *Al-Ṣaḥīḥ* by Muhammad ibn Ḥibbān al-Bustī, *Ṣaḥīḥ* by Ibn Khuzaymah, and *Al-Maṣābīḥ* by Abū Muhammad Ḥusayn ibn Masʿūd al-Baghawī who revived the Sunnah and repelled deviation.

To this rich list of books may be added *Mishkāt al-Maṣābīḥ* by Muhammad ibn ʿAbdullāh al-Khaṭīb al-Tabrīzī (d. 737 AH). This book has also been included in curricula of Ḥadīth studies, and has received good commentaries and annotations particularly in the Indian sub-continent. It has been brought to light and received its due attention through books written on the history of Ḥadīth writing and documentation, biographies and encyclopaedias.

Disciplines Introduced to Serve Ḥadīth

For the preservation of the Prophet's Ḥadīth and to prevent doubts being raised about its status and position, God has guided the Muslim community to formulate disciplines and methodologies which could serve only what God loves to be preserved so that its benefit continues one generation after another. These include:

1. ʿIlm Muṣṭalaḥ al-Ḥadīth (Ḥadīth Terminology)

Scholars have written down the rules and principles they have formulated for sorting out authentic *aḥādīth*. They classify ḥadīth under three main headings, leading to the formulation of the Ḥadīth Terminology discipline, or *ʿĪlm Muṣṭalaḥ al-ḥadīth.* This discipline lays down methodological rules for the verification and authentication of reports. It is the most accurate methodology ever known in history for establishing true reporting.

ʿIlm Muṣṭalaḥ al-Ḥadīth classifies reports into authentic or *ṣaḥīḥ*, acceptable or *ḥasan*, and poor or *ḍaʿīf*, and each of these is sub-divided into a number of categories. It outlines definite conditions concerning reporters and what is reported, and explains the inconsistencies and defects that affect reports, the reasons for rejecting reports or putting them aside until other factors come about to support them. It provides details of how the ḥadīth is learnt from scholars, and how it is transmitted and checked, as well as the manners to be observed by Ḥadīth scholars and students. All such matters were previously dealt with in separate areas, or were merely entertained or practised by scholars during the first three generations. Subsequently scholars dealt with these in their specialized works, following the same pattern of development in other Islamic sciences.

Books written on *Muṣṭalaḥ al-Ḥadīth* which have proved very useful when they were incorporated in the curricula of Islamic studies in the Indian sub-continent include *Nukhbat al-Fikar fī Muṣṭalaḥ Ahl al-Athar*, and its annotation, *Nuzhat al-Naẓar*. Both books are by Imām Aḥmad ibn ʿAlī ibn Ḥajar al-ʿAsqalānī (d. 852 AH)

2. *ʿIlm al-Jarḥ wal-Taʿdīl* (Grading of Reporters)

Another result of these blessed efforts is *ʿIlm al-Jarḥ wal-Taʿdīl*, also known as *ʿIlm Mīzān al-Rijāl* which is a discipline concerned with the reporters of ḥadīth, their integrity, reliability, acceptability, accuracy of reporting, etc. It is an important branch of study borne out of the scholarly efforts of Ḥadīth specialists unparalleled in the history of any other nation. What gave rise to this discipline was the keen interest of Ḥadīth scholars to give accurate grading to ḥadīth reporters in order to establish the grade of every reported ḥadīth. Scholars used to test their own contemporaries and inquire about earlier reporters, declaring their verdicts about each one without hesitation, because, to them, this was part of ensuring that only authentic *aḥādīth* are attributed to the Prophet.

3. *Fann Asmā' al-Rijāl* (Reporters' Names)

Scholarly efforts to serve the study of Ḥadīth also gave special attention to the identification of ḥadīth reporters and transmitters. Scholars wanted to know the names of each reporter, their ancestry, the main events in their lives, their characters, truthfulness and how good their memories were. Thus, while God promised His Messenger that he would continue to be remembered with great respect by future generations, people who had a direct link with the Prophet's heritage became themselves subject to study by later scholars. They are now remembered with affection and respect, which is a blessing they have received through the service they gave to Ḥadīth.

So, a new discipline with the name *Asmā' al-Rijāl* came into being as a unique branch of study, one which the Muslim community is right to feel very proud of. It is indeed unique to Islam. In his English introduction to *Al-Isābah fī Aḥwāl al-Ṣaḥābah* by Ibn Ḥajar, Dr Sprenger writes: 'No community has ever been successful in establishing a discipline similar to that of *Asmā' al-Rijāl*, which has given us the biography of no less than five hundred thousand people.'

Ḥadīth scholars were not only interested in grading the ḥadīth reporters. They were committed to establish the truth about them and to state it in all honesty. Therefore, they collected whatever information they could about the character, habits, morality and manners of each reporter, and whatever is relevant to assigning to each of them their grades of reliability, such as how accurate and meticulous they were in their reporting, piety, knowledge and memory, etc. They also collected what the contemporaries of each reporter said about him, fearing no one and making no allowances for anyone, even though he may be a powerful prince or an eminent scholar. There are numerous anecdotes that testify to the accuracy of these scholars and their painstaking efforts in this regard, as well as their commitment to the truth. In this, their work was a practical implementation of the divine order:

يَـٰٓأَيُّهَا ٱلَّذِينَ ءَامَنُوا۟ كُونُوا۟ قَوَّٰمِينَ بِٱلْقِسْطِ شُهَدَآءَ لِلَّهِ
وَلَوْ عَلَىٰٓ أَنفُسِكُمْ أَوِ ٱلْوَٰلِدَيْنِ وَٱلْأَقْرَبِينَ ۚ ... ﴿١٣٥﴾

'*Believers! Be ever steadfast in upholding equity, bearing witness to the truth for the sake of God, even though it be against yourselves, or your parents and kin.*' [Al-Nisā' 4: 135].

Comparative *Fiqh*

Legal or *Fiqh* differences and different rulings and views led to a need to compare approaches and rulings advanced by schools and scholars in the light of the Qur'an and the Sunnah generally, and in the light of *aḥādīth* of different grades in particular, so as to give more weight to a particular school or view. This task was undertaken by scholars of different schools, particularly the four main schools of law, and by specialized Ḥadīth scholars. They wrote books on comparative *Fiqh,* showing how to weigh up different rulings and views on the same issue. These books reflect their authors' broad vision, profound knowledge and accurate quotations. We make no claim that all such books are free of bias or favouritism, which may be unintentional. It is not to be expected that any scholarly endeavour can be free of such bias. But such books on comparative *Fiqh* are very useful.

Ḥadīth Dictionaries and Glossaries

Ḥadīth scholars across different periods produced dictionaries and glossaries to explain terms and individual words that occur in the text of different *aḥādīth*. Scholars have taken care to explain such words in their books of commentary on ḥadīth collections. For example, al-ʿAynī's *ʿUmdat al-Qārī*, a voluminous commentary on al-Bukhārī's *Ṣaḥīḥ* and al-Nawawī's commentary on Muslim's *Ṣaḥīḥ*. But the scholar who achieved special eminence in this area, which is highly important in understanding the Ḥadīth and implementing it, was Muhammad Ṭāhir al-Fattanī (d. 986 AH), an Indian scholar from the state of Gujurat. He wrote *Majmaʿ Biḥār al-Anwār fī Ghrā'ib al-Tanzīl wa Laṭā'if al-Akhbār*, a 5-volume work which is indispensable for any teacher and student of Ḥadīth.

To make the value and importance of this book clear, we need only to quote a couple of sentences of its evaluation by an eminent Ḥadīth scholar, the historian ʿAbd al-Ḥayy al-Ḥasanī (d. 1341 AH) in his 8-volume work, *Nuzhat al-Khawāṭir wa Bahjat al-Masāmiʿ wal-Nawāẓir*, which is a biographical encyclopaedia on Indian personalities. When he speaks about Muhammad Ṭāhir al-Fattanī in Volume 4, he says:

> 'He included in his book all the unfamiliar things in Ḥadīth and what has been written about it. It serves as a commentary on the six authentic collections. It has been universally accepted by scholars ever since its publication. Indeed, all scholars are indebted to him for this priceless work.'

The Need for the Sunnah Today

We have spoken at length on the fact that the Ḥadīth is an accurate standard to evaluate the practical life of the Muslim community at any time. Indeed the Ḥadīth is a powerful tool to pinpoint the weaknesses of any Muslim community.

It provides the education necessary for reformers. We have also mentioned how history provides a clear testimony of the effectiveness of Ḥadīth and the Sunnah in encouraging revival and reform.[23]

It clearly appears that those who advocate that we should follow in the footsteps of Western civilization (sometimes partly, but far more often completely) have realized, by intelligence and experience, that the Ḥadīth is the most difficult obstacle in their way. It is the Ḥadīth that directly runs contrary to their desires and ideas, as well as to their way of life. It undermines their efforts or makes them completely useless, putting up the most difficult of challenges for them to overcome. Hence, they regard the Ḥadīth as their most important opponent. It is the one force that blocks their attempts to move the present Muslim generation from one civilization to another. They want the Muslim community to abandon its way of life based on Islamic teachings, and the Prophet's example and guidance which God urges us in the Qur'an to follow.

لَّقَدْ كَانَ لَكُمْ فِي رَسُولِ ٱللَّهِ أُسْوَةٌ حَسَنَةٌ ... ﴿٢١﴾

"*Surely, in God's Messenger you have a good example for everyone who looks forward to God and the Last Day, and remembers God frequently.*" [Al-Aḥzāb 33: 21].

قُلْ إِن كُنتُمْ تُحِبُّونَ ٱللَّهَ فَٱتَّبِعُونِي يُحْبِبْكُمُ ٱللَّهُ وَيَغْفِرْ لَكُمْ ذُنُوبَكُمْ ۗ
وَٱللَّهُ غَفُورٌ رَّحِيمٌ ﴿٣١﴾

"*Say: If you love God, follow me; God will love you and forgive you your sins.*" [Āl 'Imrān 3: 31].

---

[23] Further discussion will be provided in the second pamphlet in the present volume.

In the Ḥadīth and the Sunnah we have confirmation of the commendation of certain manners, values and practices which the Prophet invites us to adopt, as well as unworthy matters the Prophet denounces, considering them part of pagan life or as imitation of un-Islamic values and practices. Hence, such people target the Ḥadīth with all their might, trying to make Muslims turn away from the Sunnah. They have used their undoubted intelligence and inside knowledge of the mentality of the Muslim community to turn the Muslims away from following the Sunnah and implementing Islamic law as the Prophet did. They want a state of unrestrained licence, indulgence, the fulfilment of all desire and the imitation of Western ways to prevail all over the Muslim world. Hence, it is important for the Muslim community in general and the advocates of Islamic revival in particular to be fully aware of the role of Ḥadīth in the promotion of an Islamic social climate and the adoption of an Islamic attitude to all life problems. This is briefly outlined in the next pamphlet in this volume.

II

Ḥadīth and the Promotion of Islamic Climate and Attitudes

CONSTITUENT ELEMENTS OF A NEW SOCIETY

The mission of Prophet Muhammad ﷺ has been the source of every good thing and the origin of all that brings human happiness. Through it, a unique religious climate came into existence, giving rise to a similarly unique Muslim community. Careful consideration of the practical methods and the means used to bring this about is bound to reveal that the key to this amazing transformation lies in the three constituent elements of the new society. These are:

1) the Qur'an;

2) the Prophet's personality, how he conducted his life and the moral values he laid down; and

3) the Prophet's teachings, directives and actions which are collectively called The Sunnah, including the Ḥadīth.

These three elements were central to the fulfilment of the objectives of the Prophet's mission, shaping a new community. In fact, without these three elements no ideal society could come into being, and no practical model could have taken shape. All three are necessary in moulding a social order which reflects Islamic beliefs, morality, practices, feelings, inclinations, common-sense, and social bonds. A practical model is necessary for a faith to come alive, for in our world one lamp is lit by another.

The Prophet's companions, and their worthy successors, have provided a shining example for us, with their profound faith, commitment to Islamic moral standards, and practical dedication to the cause of Islam. All this did not come about as a result of only reciting God's book and understanding it. An equally important factor was the splendid ideal they saw in their midst, giving directives, setting standards of morality and behaviour, and providing practical guidance that ensured a life of peace and happiness for all. All this was characteristic of Islamic life during the time of the Prophet (peace be upon him).

Perfect Islamic Life

These factors formulated a refined Islamic sense which is not confined to observing the rules set and working within specified controls. These were complemented with sound motivation and practical modalities, enhanced by a spirit of pure devotion, and strengthened by a keen desire to fulfil duties and give everyone their rights. Indeed they were cultivated with a refined sense of purity and morality.

The standard-setting generation of early Muslims read the Qur'anic orders to attend to prayers, and appreciated the praise the Qur'an gave to believers

ٱلَّذِينَ هُمْ فِى صَلَاتِهِمْ خَٰشِعُونَ ﴿٢﴾

> "*Who humble themselves in their prayer.*" [Al-Mu'minūn 23: 2].

But they did not truly understand the proper way of praying until they offered their prayers with the Prophet ﷺ and saw how he conducted himself when he bowed and prostrated himself in prayer. They described his weeping when he prayed: it was as though

> "his inside gave a sound similar to that of a boiling pan." (Related by Abū Dāwūd and al-Tirmidhī).

They learnt from the Qur'an that prayer was a believer's favourite preoccupation, but they could not appreciate how a true believer longs for the time of prayer until they heard God's Messenger say:

> "Prayer is the apple of my eye."

He expresses his dear love of prayer as he addresses Bilāl, his main caller to prayer:

> "Call the prayer, Bilāl, so that we may have our comforting solace."

They recognized the deep relation between the mosque and a believer's heart as they contemplated the Prophet's statement enumerating seven categories of good believers who will enjoy God's protection on the Day of Judgement. One of these is

> "a person whose heart always inclines to mosques."

They knew how much the Qur'an encouraged supplication, inviting people to be insistent in their prayer, time after time, and criticising those who felt too proud to pray to God to grant their requests. They certainly knew the meaning of prayer and supplication, but they did not appreciate it fully until they saw the Prophet ﷺ placing his forehead on the ground in Badr and repeating an earnest supplication, saying:

> "My Lord! I appeal to You for the fulfilment of Your promise. My Lord! If it is Your wish, You would not be worshipped on earth." (Related by al-Bukhārī).

They also witnessed his anxiety that perturbed Abu-Bakr ﷺ so much as to say to the Prophet that he had prayed enough, and that God was sure to answer his prayers.

The Prophet's companions were aware that the fundamental thing about prayer and supplication is to say it in earnest, acknowledging one's complete submission to God and total inability to benefit oneself without God's help. When supplication is manifestly characterized by such acknowledgement, it is more valuable and more likely to be answered. But they did not fully appreciate the true sense of submission to God and acknowledging one's weakness and lack of resources, making a passionate appeal to God, until they heard the Prophet ﷺ pray in Arafat:

> "My Lord! You hear my words and see me in my position. You know my secret and what I do in public. Nothing of what I say, do or feel is hidden from You. I am only a poor, helpless, afraid sinner who appeals to You for help. I pray as a helpless, humble sinner, and appeal to You like a forlorn, sorrow-stricken servant of Yours. I hang down my head before You; let my tears flow in awe of You; and humble myself before You. Let not my prayers go unheard. Be gracious to me. Yours is the best succour to be sought, and You are the most bountiful." (Related in *Kanz al-ʿUmmāl* on Ibn ʿAbbās's authority).

Qur'anic Morality

The Prophet's companions read in the Qur'an that this present life provides only fleeting comforts, and that it is the life to come that should be sought after. They understood the Qur'anic statement:

وَمَا هَٰذِهِ ٱلْحَيَوٰةُ ٱلدُّنْيَآ إِلَّا لَهْوٌ وَلَعِبٌ ۚ وَإِنَّ ٱلدَّارَ ٱلْءَاخِرَةَ
لَهِىَ ٱلْحَيَوَانُ ۚ لَوْ كَانُوا۟ يَعْلَمُونَ ﴿٦٤﴾

> "*The life of this world is nothing but a passing delight and a play; whereas the life in the hereafter is indeed the only true life, if they but knew it.*" [Al-'Ankabūt 29: 64].

But they only witnessed how this applied in practice when they saw the way the Prophet ﷺ conducted his own life. They were able then to appreciate how those who set higher store by the life to come should conduct their life in this world, and how their families should live. They not only saw the Prophet's practical example, but they also listened to him as he described the terrible suffering endured by people whose actions incur for them punishment in hell and, by contrast, the great happiness enjoyed by those whose actions earn them admittance into heaven. Thus they felt a mixture of fear and aspiration, as though they actually saw both heaven and hell with their very own eyes.

Similarly, they knew the meaning of words like mercy, humility, kindness, morality and similar ones used in divine instructions and directives. These were words of their own language. They fully understood the Qur'an. But they did not appreciate the broad scope of these and similar words and how they are properly applied in practical life until they saw how the Prophet ﷺ treated the weak, handicapped, women, children, orphans, the poor and the elderly, as well as his own friends, companions, servants and members of his own household, and listened to his admonition and his directives. They understood Qur'anic instructions about the fulfilment of duties towards the Muslim community in general, but there are forms and practices that relate to such fulfilment which are rarely considered by people and, even if considered, are rarely appreciated. These include practices like visiting the sick, taking part in funerals and blessing a person after he sneezes.

In the Qur'an we read firm instructions about certain values including perfecting one's behaviour, dealing kindly with those who are entitled to certain rights, and being kindly and dutiful to parents. I wonder whether, when considering dutifulness to parents and kindness to relations, any professors of ethics, educationalists or psychologists could have set their sights as high as the summit indicated by the following ḥadīth:

> "It is one of the best types of dutifulness to parents that a person should extend a favour to the friends and relations of his father after he has passed away." (Related by Muslim).

What ingenious mind could have attained the sublime level of devoted loyalty that the following report suggests:

> "Sometimes the Prophet might have a sheep slaughtered, and then he would cut it into pieces and send a piece each to the old friends of his late wife, Khadījah."

These are only a few of the great many examples cited in the ethical and social sections of anthologies of Ḥadīth. They suggest the importance the Prophet attached to different aspects of life and his new teachings concerning such aspects. In all this, the Prophet's *aḥādīth* provide an invaluable treasure house of knowledge for all humanity.

The Right Climate

Injunctions and commandments, regardless of religion or community, are not sufficient to impart to any activity a healthy atmosphere and sound form so as to make them effective and influential. Thus, an order to attend regularly to prayers will not, on its own, create the appropriate mental attitude to prayers, nor will it generate the necessary environment to establish and maintain prayers. Nor is it sufficient to help produce the spiritual, psychological, social, moral and religious effects of prayer. To achieve this a host of principles, rules, directives and teachings are needed to add to the value of prayer and make it more inspiring and effective. Hence, the Qur'an made ablution and cleanliness prerequisites for prayer, and emphasized the need for full awareness, humility, calmness and sincerity during prayer and recommended that it should be offered in congregation.

Needless to say, the more carefully and meticulously these external formalities are observed the better will prayer generate its spiritual, social and moral effects. Those who study the Ḥadīth and the Prophet's life recognize that the Prophet's practical example, guidance and teachings have made a priceless contribution which makes prayer an even better and more effective instrument in self-purification, moral and spiritual perfection and sincere devotion. In addition, the Prophet's guidance enhances the effectiveness of prayer in providing people with the right perspective that attaches proper value to the life hereafter in relation to the life of this world. Furthermore, with the Prophet's guidance prayer plays a greater role in educating the Muslim community and strengthening its sense of unity and solidarity.

Take for example the emphasis placed on properly formulating one's intention to perform the ablutions, and how one should be conscious of this before starting. Take also the reward promised for walking to the mosque; the supplication one says on the way; the manners to be observed on entering the mosque; the recommended prayer in greeting to the mosque; the voluntary prayers recommended to be offered regularly; and the reward for waiting in the mosque till the prayer is called; the multiple reward given for congregational prayers; the reward earned by calling for prayer and the call to start it; and the great emphasis attached to leading congregational prayer; and the set of rules that apply to it; the emphatic requirement to follow the Imam in every action throughout the prayer; ensuring that all rows are straight; the special position accorded to educational circles in the mosque; the circles engaged in God's glorification; the manners to be observed when leaving the mosque and the supplication said at the time, etc. Needless to say, when such good manners and recommendations are observed, prayers become far more effective in purifying people's hearts and souls, cultivating sound morality and good manners, and strengthening people's relationship with God.

Add to all this the exceptional importance the Ḥadīth attaches to relating how the Prophet offered his prayers; how fond he was of offering voluntary prayers; and how absorbed he was when he recited the Qur'an. Reflect now on how far observing all such values improves the prayers of the Muslim community and what sort of psychological and spiritual climate they create. The same may be said about fasting, zakat, pilgrimage and the manners that should be observed when offering these obligatory acts of worship. What is most important is to learn what the Prophet said about them and how he approached them practically. We need also to reflect a little on how effective and beneficial these duties would be if they were stripped of the manners and complements the *aḥādīth* detail, removing them from the climate generated by the Prophet's statements concerning them. How far would they then be effective in raising people's spirits, enhancing their determination and consolidating their moral attitude to strengthen their community which is refined by the values of devotion and pure worship of God?

The fact remains that the practical example given by the Prophet and his directives generate the climate in which the tree of faith could grow and yield its fruits. Religion is not a hard set of restraints and controls. It does not come alive without passion, the right spirit and a practical example. The best and most reliable collection of these is what is outlined in Ḥadīth anthologies, which form a unique feature of the Muslim community. No other community or group of followers of any prophet, nor the followers of any divine religion, of whatever race or place, have anything akin to the authentic Ḥadīth collections.

The History of Earlier Prophets

Earlier religions, including Judaism, Christianity, Zoroastrianism, Buddhism and Brahmanism lost their vigour and spirit over a short period of time and were no longer able to retain their purity and survive, let alone grow and flourish. The main reason for this is that none of these religions managed to retain reliable accounts of the life of their prophets. It is such accurate and reliable accounts that give the impetus to renewing faith and reviving spiritual strength. None of these faiths managed to retain the sort of spiritual climate that helps their adherents' spiritual growth and ability to resist material temptation.

Yet they felt the need for such reliable accounts, which is only natural. Having no reliable sources, they could only fill the vacuum with stories of the life of some prominent figures among the followers of their religions, such as priests. These provide accounts of what they said on different occasions, and what sort of teachings they emphasized.

This was the reason behind the compilation of Talmudic literature[24] which caught the fancy of the Jews who gave much attention to studying and explaining the Talmud, which was soon to relegate the Pentateuch to a position of secondary importance. Indeed, a number of prominent Jewish religious figures have stated that the Talmud takes precedence over the Old Testament. The Talmud, however, reflects a fragile Jewish mentality that is easily influenced by external factors. Hence, it contains much that has no sound basis, and some insupportable legends and superstitions. These remind us of the Qur'anic verse that states:

وَمَا قَدَرُوا۟ ٱللَّهَ حَقَّ قَدْرِهِۦٓ ... ﴿٩١﴾

"*No true understanding of God have they.*" [Al-An'ām 6: 91].

---

[24] The Talmud is the standard collection of texts and commentaries on Jewish religious law, developed from the Pentateuch. It consists of two parts: the Mishnah and Gemara. The former is a commentary on the matters dealt with in Mosaic legislation, and the latter a commentary on the Mishnah itself. Among Orthodox Jewry the authority of the Talmud is held second only to that of the Old Testament, but according to the *Jewish Encyclopaedia*, (Vol. 11 p. 569 & Vol. 12, p. 690) the Talmud shows that polytheism held great attraction for the Jewish people.

In turn, the Christians made additions to the New Testament, such as the Acts of the Apostles, the Epistles of Paul, Peter and John, and also the Revelations of St. John.

Hindus have long revered the *Gita*, which contains the sayings and sermons of Sri Krishna. Added to this are two more religious books, namely the *Ramayana*, a record of the life history of Sri Ram Chandra, and the *Mahabharata* which is an epic of ancient India. The same is true of the Zoroastrians who rever the *Avesta*, and its priestly commentaries known as the *Vendidah* and the *Bundahish*.

None of these scriptures were able to bring back these old religions to the teachings of their original advocates, or to provide a model of their lives, practices and directives which would encourage people to follow their lead. Nor could they foster any keen desire to safeguard the beliefs and traditions of the founders of these faiths. Indeed they did more harm than good. These books distorted the religious thinking of their followers, encouraged excessive adoration of different beings, elevating them to the rank of deities, and promoted superstitious beliefs. Furthermore, they have had a profound influence on the language, literature, culture and social traditions of their followers. They gradually turned these religions into a mixture of superstition, mythical lore, deceptive reasoning and new extremist interpretations in which the original teachings constitute no more than a drop in the ocean.

Biographies of Prophets

The dire lack of correct biographies of the prophets who founded the religions of old is an indisputable fact. A comparative study of Prophet Muhammad's biography and Ḥadīth anthologies containing his authentic statements on the one hand and the chronicles of earlier prophets on the other, is bound to give amazing results. Most of the latter have been lost due to ignorance, carelessness or natural and man-made catastrophes. These religions fulfilled their roles over a short period of time, with the early generations following the guidance of their prophets. But they felt no need to preserve such heritage for posterity.

Take for example the life of Jesus Christ (peace be upon him), God's messenger, who preceded Prophet Muhammad ﷺ, the last of all God's messengers. In him believes a great community with marvellous achievements in research and scholarship. Their love of their prophet has been so great that they raised him to the level of Lordship. Nevertheless, they have been able to provide only a sketchy picture of Jesus that cannot offer a complete model, providing complete life guidance for the individual or the community. Until recently, the general Christian thinking maintained that the New Testament provides a chronicle of the last three years of the Christ's life. Christian researchers and experts have more recently concluded that the total span of events pertaining to the life of Jesus Christ narrated in the Gospels add up to no more than fifty days of his life.

A contributor to the *Encyclopaedia Britannica,* Rev. Dr Charles Anderson Scott, writes in his article on Jesus:

> The attempt to write a 'life of Jesus' should frankly be abandoned. The material for it certainly does not exist. It has been calculated that the total number of days of his life regarding which we have any record does not exceed 50.[25]

---

[25] *Encyclopaedia Britannica*, 14th edition, Vol. XIII, pp. 16-17. Another scholar, Albert Schweitzer, who has surveyed the whole enterprise from the earliest to modern times about the life of Jesus Christ in his monumental work *The Quest of Historical Jesus* begins the first chapter with the words: 'There is nothing more negative than the result of the critical study of the life of Jesus.'

As for other prophets and leading figures of earlier religions, it can be safely said that their life accounts are buried under the huge heap of forgotten history. Major episodes of their lives that are fundamentally essential to give a proper picture that could serve as a role model have been irrevocably lost. This is both logical and consistent with divine will. Historical figures provide shining examples for others over a limited period of time. When such a period is over, there is little benefit in preserving them over future generations. By contrast, what continues to be needed will survive unaltered, yielding its benefit generation after generation.

The case of Islam and the life of the Prophet ﷺ who delivered the Islamic message provide a totally different example. The clarity and reliability of its details cannot be greater. It is so unlike the chronicles of great historical figures, including prophets. A glance at Ḥadīth anthologies, accounts of the Prophet's character, and also the Prophet's biographies and books devoted to his military expeditions, will confirm what we have just said. Anyone who examines the *aḥādīth* recorded in the authentic anthologies on the Prophet's pilgrimage will learn, for example, how Prophet Muhammad ﷺ used perfume before entering into the state of consecration, or *iḥrām*, who gave him this perfume, and what type of perfume it was. He will also know in accurate detail how the Prophet marked his sacrificial animals,[26] what the marks were like, on which side of these animals they were placed, and how he wiped off their blood. He

[26] One of the duties of pilgrimage is to sacrifice one sheep or more. A pilgrim who brings his sacrifice with him may mark it with a superficial scratch, so that no one will harm the animal until its time for sacrifice in Mina. – Editor's note

will also learn how the Prophet was cupped on the way, on what part of his body, and the location on the way where this was done. He can also determine the places where he rested en route from Madinah to Makkah, and count the days of his journey. Needless to say, all this took place at a time when people kept no diaries and made no records of events. Nevertheless, we have a detailed record of such events, to the extent that we know of a snake passing nearby and how it managed to escape. We learn the names of everyone who rode behind the Prophet on his camel on this journey.[27] We know the name of the person who shaved the Prophet's head at the end of his consecration, or *iḥrām*, how he divided his hair, who shaved his right side and who his left side. Needless to say, a detailed record has been preserved of his speeches at Arafat and in Mina, as well as all that he enjoined. This was done in fulfilment of his directive:

> 'Those who are present should convey what they have heard me say to those who are absent. A person learning in this way may be better aware of its import than one who has heard it directly."

Western writers have acknowledged this fact. In his biography of the Prophet entitled *An Apology for Mohammad and the Qur'an,* John Davenport writes:

> "Of all law-makers and conquerors there is not one the events of whose life are more true and more detailed than those of the Prophet Muhammad."[28]

---

[27] The author of *Nasīm al-Riyāḍ* mentions by name 38 of the Prophet's companions who rode behind him on his camel on different occasions. Ibn Mandah mentions a higher figure.

[28] Cited by Syed Sulaiman Nadwi, *Muhammad: the Ideal Prophet*, p. 98 [Arabic edition].

R. Bosworth Smith, former fellow of Trinity College of Oxford delivered a series of lectures on "Muhammad and Muhammadanism" under the auspices of the Royal Institution of Great Britain in February and March 1874. He says in his lectures, which were later enlarged and published under the same title:

> What is true of religions, generally, is also true, unfortunately, of those three religions which I have called, for want of a better name, historical, and their founders. We know all too little of the first and earliest labourers; too much, perhaps, of those who have entered into their labours. We know less of Zoroaster and Confucius than we do of Solon and Socrates; less of Moses and Buddha than we do of Ambrose and Augustine. We know indeed of some fragments of Christ's life: who can lift the veil of thirty years that prepared the way for the three? What we do know indeed has renovated a third of the world, and may yet renovate much more; an ideal of life at once remote and near; possible and impossible, but how much we do not know! What do we know of his mother, of his home life, of his early friends, of his relation to them, of the gradual dawning, or, it may be, the sudden revelation, of his divine message? How many questions about him occur to each of us which must always remain questions?
>
> But in Muhammadanism everything is different; here instead of the shadowy and the mysterious we have history. We know as much of Muhammad as we do even of Luther and Milton. The mythical, the legendary, the supernatural is almost wanting in the original Arab authorities, or at all events can easily be distinguished from what is historical. Nobody here is

in doubt of himself or of others; there is the full light of day upon that that light can ever reach at all.[29]

Fair Judgement Criterion

The Ḥadīth constitutes an accurate scale and a perfect criterion by which reformers can evaluate people's practices and identify any deviation from the proper norms in public life. Maintaining a proper standard of morality and fair practice can only be achieved through the Qur'an when supplemented by the Ḥadīth. It is the Ḥadīth that fills the vacuum caused by the Prophet passing away. Such a vacuum is perfectly normal:

وَمَا مُحَمَّدٌ إِلَّا رَسُولٌ قَدْ خَلَتْ مِن قَبْلِهِ الرُّسُلُ ... ﴿١٤٤﴾

"*Muhammad is only a messenger: all messengers have passed away before him...*" [Āl 'Imrān 3: 144].

إِنَّكَ مَيِّتٌ وَإِنَّهُم مَّيِّتُونَ ﴿٣٠﴾

"*You shall certainly die; and they shall certainly die.*" [Al-Zumar 39: 30].

Had it not been for the *aḥādīth* which represent a well balanced way of life, the Prophet's sound directives and his rulings on questions faced by the Muslim community, the balance would have tilted. Should it lose the practical example of the Prophet, which God has commanded us to follow, the Muslim community would suffer an imbalance resulting from either a too strict or a too liberal approach. God says in the Qur'an:

---

[29] Cited in Nadwi, ibid, English edition, Lucknow, 1976, pp. 66-67.

لَّقَدْ كَانَ لَكُمْ فِي رَسُولِ ٱللَّهِ أُسْوَةٌ حَسَنَةٌ ... ﴿٢١﴾

"*In God's Messenger, you have a good example to follow.*" [Al-Aḥzāb 33: 21].

قُلْ إِن كُنتُمْ تُحِبُّونَ ٱللَّهَ فَٱتَّبِعُونِي يُحْبِبْكُمُ ٱللَّهُ وَيَغْفِرْ لَكُمْ ذُنُوبَكُمْ ۗ
وَٱللَّهُ غَفُورٌ رَّحِيمٌ ﴿٣١﴾

"*Say: If you love God, follow me; God will love you and forgive you your sins.*" [Āl 'Imrān 3: 31].

It is indeed the Prophet who is the perfect example for us to emulate. Following his example provides us with strength and confidence, and facilitates our way to implement Islamic rules in an easy and relaxed way.

Motivation for Reform

The Prophet's *aḥādīth* constitute a source of strength that is full of life, motivating reform and renewal. It has always urged the need to fight corruption and deviation, providing social checks and balances in all Muslim generations and communities. It is the standard by which all deviation, superstition and un-Islamic customs are rejected. It shows the way to maintaining the true way of Islam. Hence, the Prophet's *aḥādīth* represent a basic need of the Muslim community, and they must be verified, recorded and published.

Ḥadīth anthologies have always been, and still are, the guiding light that formulates correct Islamic thinking within the Muslim community. Through Ḥadīth, reformers in different generations received proper Islamic education and clear Islamic thought. It provided them with the right arguments to pursue their efforts for reforming their communities and eradicating deviation and corruption. Anyone who strives to return his community to the true and pure model of Islam finds the *aḥādīth* indispensable because they provide the link between any Muslim community and the model of life provided by the Prophet. Similarly indispensable is the Ḥadīth for anyone who needs to deduce rulings on new questions and life problems.

Historical Evidence

Islamic history provides strong evidence confirming all this. Whenever Muslims lost sight of the importance of *aḥādīth* and neglected their links with Ḥadīth anthologies and with the Sunnah in general, there crept into their life some alien practices and foreign traditions. This is true despite the presence of a good number of advocates who call on people to follow divine guidance, urge spiritual purification and sound morality, as well as great Islamic scholars in all specializations. Indeed it is true even when Muslims live in powerful and affluent states. The introduction of such alien practices could gradually lead the Muslim community to a situation whereby it is not much different from a *jāhiliyyah* society. This confirms the Prophet's warning:

> "You shall follow in the footsteps of communities that have gone by, copying their example in detail." (Related by al-Ḥākim).

Take for instance the religious and social conditions of the Indian Muslims during the tenth century of the Islamic era when religious and intellectual circles in the subcontinent had almost severed themselves from the Ḥadīth and its authentic sources. In that period, they had no contact with the centres of religious learning in Hijaz, Yemen, Egypt and Syria where the study of Ḥadīth was still pursued. Institutions of religious education in India at the time concentrated on learning the school of Islamic law that prevailed in that country, putting much effort into studying its books, commentaries, methodologies, etc. Soon deviation crept in with unsound practices and alien usages gaining popularity. New forms of worship were invented, such as a complimentary prostration before mystic Shaykhs or at their graves, lighting candles at sepulchral monuments, offering prayers before graves as though they were mosques, fasting and offering sacrifices to propitiate saints, and holding fairs to commemorate their birth and death anniversaries.

Such were the prevailing conditions when God brought forth reformers and well versed scholars, such as Aḥmad ibn ʿAbd al-Aḥad Sirhindi (d. 1034 AH 1625 CE) who denounced all un-Islamic practices in clear terms. He refuted the notion of virtuous deviation, or *bidʿat ḥasanah*, showing that it is totally unacceptable. He also denounced in the strongest of terms the creed of pantheism, or *waḥdat al-wujūd*, calling on people to follow only the Prophet's example and shun all alien practices. In one of his memorable remarks he said:

> What we require is the testimony of Muhammad of Arabia (peace be upon him), not that of Muhiyuddin ibn Arabi or Sadr al-Din Qunawi or Abd al-Razzaq al-Kashi. We need the authentic texts and the practical example of Madinah, not the words Ibn Arabi wrote in his books.[30]

---

[30] *Mukatabat Imam Rabbani*, Vol. II, Letter No. 100. This is a free translation as the original text makes contextual references that will not be easily understood except by a reader with the right background. – Editor's note.

Sirhindi's contemporary, Shaykh ʿAbd al-Ḥaqq ibn Sayf al-Dīn al-Bukharī of Delhi (d. 1052 AH/ 1642 CE) spent his whole life in the teaching and propagation of Ḥadīth in India. Following in their footsteps, Shah Waliyullāh (d. 1176 AH/ 1762 CE) and his worthy sons and students took up the cause of teaching and preaching the Qur'an and the Ḥadīth. They explained the true concepts of Islam, advocating a return to the pure Islamic faith. They taught the six authentic Ḥadīth anthologies, known as *al-Ṣiḥāḥ al-Sittah*, giving them a prominent place in their curriculum which helped to make India, remote as it is from the cultural centres of Islam, a seat of learning attracting students of Ḥadīth from all over the Muslim world.

One of the most extensive and powerful revivalist movements in the Muslim world in the thirteenth century of the Islamic calendar sprang up in India. One need only read the history of the two martyrs Sayyid Aḥmad ibn ʿIrfān and Muhammad Ismāʿīl (d. 1246 AH) to learn about this great reformist movement that changed the very character of the land and its people, giving new life to the Muslims of the subcontinent and bringing back images from the life of early Muslim generations. This reformist movement was able to revive many of the practices of the Prophet which had long been abandoned. It uprooted many deviant practices, superstitions and pagan traditions which had previously taken hold in Indian society.

I am absolutely certain that without the authentic Ḥadīth anthologies, Muslims would have never been able to revive the Sunnah of the Prophet, distinguishing it from deviant practices. None of the great scholars that adorned Islamic history with their revivalist and reformist efforts, from with Ibn Taymiyyah (d. 728 AH/ 1328 CE) to Muhammad ibn ʿAbd al-Wahhāb (d. 1206 AH/ 1792 CE), would have been able to play any significant role without them. Nor would their contemporaries and followers of revivalist scholars such as Muhammad ibn ʿAli al-Shawkānī (d. 1255 AH/ 1839 CE), Muhammad ibn Ismāʿīl al-Sanʿānī (d. 1182 AH/ 1768 CE), Ahmad ibn ʿAbdullāh ibn Idrīs al-Ḥasanī (d. 1293 AH/ 1876 CE) ʿAbdullāh Ghaznavi of Amritsar, Muhammad Aʿẓam of Kabul (d. 1298 AH/ 1872 CE), Ḥusayn ʿAlī al-Wānī (d. 1363 AH/ 1935), Ghulām Rasūl (d. 1291 AH/ 1865 CE) and many others.

The same story can be told of many Arab and Muslim countries, such as Iraq, Syria, Egypt, Tunisia, Algeria, Morocco, Afghanistan and Turkistan. However, I have limited myself to India for brevity and because I know it at first hand.

A Permanent Record

A phenomenon that attests to the truth of Islam as the final divine message for all mankind is that, unlike the followers of old religions, Muslims were never intellectually isolated from their faith and its practical implementation. The Prophet's *aḥādīth* have given them a permanent record of the spiritual and religious climate enjoyed by the Prophet's companions, and how Islam moulded their spiritual and practical life. This enables every Muslim generation to instantly recall that climate enlightened by the presence of the Prophet, seeing how he addressed his companions and how they listened attentively to him and took immediate action to implement his teachings. Not only so, but we can also learn what feelings and emotions they experienced. Thus, we are able today to identify the pattern of actions and manners faith produces and the type of life generated by firm belief in the life to come.

Thus, this permanent record gives us a complete picture of life in the Prophet's family home: what he did at night and how his family lived. We see him in front of us, prostrating himself in complete devotion, sending his earnest prayers and addressing God with sincere humility. When we look at him in his night worship, his eyes tearful, his feet swollen from long standing in prayer, and then hear his answer to his wife who wonders why he worships so much when God has granted him forgiveness of any sin he might ever commit:

> "Should I not be, then, a grateful servant of God?" (Related by al-Bukhārī and Muslim).

Looking at him in this way, how could we allow ourselves to slacken or be heedless? When we realize that month after month passes by with no fire for cooking lit in his home, and when we see him wrapping two stones over his abdomen to reduce the pangs of hunger; or lying on a hard mat that leaves its mark on his back; or refusing to go to bed at night until he has distributed among his poor companions the amount of gold and silver he received that day; or in his final illness when his family had to borrow oil to light the lamp for him; – when we see all these pictures and many more, how can we overlook the fact that no material luxury in this life is of any importance? Moreover, when we see how he attended to his family's needs, cared for the young, overlooked the faults of servants, and how he treated his companions with kindness, and his enemies with forbearance, what humanitarian lesson can we learn from anyone else?

A Full Record

It is not only the Prophet's personality that we look up to in order to capture the climate that prevailed in that unique period of history. The doors of his companions are open wide for us to have a panoramic view of life in a model Islamic society. We see them spending much of their nights in worship, while during the day they are fully dedicated soldiers serving the cause of Islam. We see them attending to their businesses, but mindful of their religious duties, frequenting mosques. We note their humility, dedication, ability to resist temptation, and complete obedience in most situations, but we also note that they made a few slips since they were only human. We see in front of our eyes how Abū Ṭalḥah provided a fine example of self-denial in order to please the Prophet. We see Kaʿb ibn Mālik staying behind at the time of the Tabūk Expedition, and how he patiently went through a hard test to prove his love of the Prophet; how he was fully committed to the cause of Islam, testifying against himself and enduring all the hardship until he won God's forgiveness. God's acceptance of his repentance is shown in conjunction with His acceptance of the Prophet's and his companions' repentance who joined him on that very expedition, so that Kaʿb would not feel left out.

We also see the unfolding of the story of falsehood that engulfed ʿĀ'ishah, the mother of believers, and witness her exceedingly delicate position, unshakable faith and model integrity before her innocence was confirmed by God Himself. We see Abū Bakr and his difficult position, his self control during this highly infuriating episode, his un-wavering trust, and resumption of extending material kindness to a man who took part in the episode that hurt him and his family so badly.

As we see all this we realize that this was a normal climate in which all sorts of events took place, leading to a whole spectrum of human attitudes, reactions, feelings and interactions. The Prophet's *aḥādīth* recorded all these, providing a clear model for successive generations to emulate.

That such a record of life at the time of the Prophet ﷺ remains preserved alongside the Qur'an and the statements of the Messenger who delivered God's message is indeed one of the unique and remarkable characteristics of Islam. No other religion benefits by such a full and permanent record. The faith that is meant to remain intact till the end of time, providing all human generations with practical examples to follow, motivating people to action, and providing nourishment for mind and heart alike must have a model social order and social climate on show. Such a model has been preserved through the Prophet's *aḥādīth*.

Ḥadīth Recording

Careful study of the recording of *aḥādīth* will show that this did not come about by coincidence. Nor was it an innovation of later generations. Indeed, the Prophet's companions took care to record the Ḥadīth during the Prophet's lifetime, when a significant number of *aḥādīth* were committed to writing. The next generation of *tabiʿīn*, or successors of the Prophet's companions, began to record and arrange *aḥādīth* towards the end of the Prophet's companions' generation. Scholars of Ḥadīth from Khurasan and Turkistan began to travel everywhere to learn, memorize and classify the *aḥādīth*, demonstrating exemplary dedication to the task in hand and benefiting by phenomenal memories. Later, scholars specialized in learning the biographies of Ḥadīth narrators, and excelled in Ḥadīth transmission. They dedicated all their time and effort to this pursuit. As a result, the whole Muslim community attached great value to Ḥadīth study in a way that has no parallel in human history. All this goes to show that it was

God's will that this practical model of Islamic life should be preserved, to serve as a guiding light for future generations. Thus, the Muslim community will continue to benefit by this spiritual, practical, and religious heritage which moulded the first Muslim generation of the Prophet's companions.

Islamic Sense and Temperament

The Muslim community not only inherited rulings and legislation, given by one generation to the next, but it also inherited the right sense, temperament, character and mentality. Thanks to the *aḥādīth*, the sense and temperament that prevailed among the Prophet's companions continued to be passed on to the next generation. Throughout Islamic history, there was no period of any considerable length when such sense and temperament were totally missing. In every generation, there were individuals who belonged in sense and personality to the Prophet's companions' generation, demonstrating similar dedication in worship, exemplary God-consciousness, straightforwardness, resolve, humility, sacrifice, giving little care to material life, looking ahead to the hereafter, fulfilling the duty of enjoining right and forbidding wrong, feeling a strong dislike of deviation and demonstrating a keen desire to follow the Prophet's Sunnah. Nothing of this could have come about without paying much attention to the study of Ḥadīth: learning, recording and teaching it, as well as writing commentaries on, and explanations of its texts, or without assigning due respect to those scholars who had a full measure of this great heritage. Indeed the Muslim community continued to pass over this legacy, with the sense and temperament it generates, from the first generation up to the present fifteenth century of the Islamic calendar, despite the strong materialistic outlook that prevails in the present generation. This great legacy continues to yield its healthy fruits.

New Motives to Reject the Sunnah

Muhammad Asad, a Western scholar who embraced Islam, explains the new trend of rejecting the Sunnah on the basis of his first hand knowledge of Western civilization and the mentality of the younger Muslim generation. He concludes that the values, standards, practices and trends of the Western civilization that is predominant in our world are basically incompatible with the Sunnah. To entertain true love of the Prophet who delivered God's message is essentially incompatible with looking up to Western civilization as the highest standard of human knowledge. This may be the reason that motivates some rulers and political figures in Arab and Muslim countries to reject the Sunnah altogether. Asad writes:

> In these days, when the influence of Western civilization makes itself more and more felt in Muslim countries, still another motive is added to the negative attitude of the so-called 'Muslim intelligentsia' in this matter. It is impossible to live according to the Sunnah of our Prophet ﷺ and to follow the Western mode of life at one and the same time. But many among the present generation of Muslims are ready to adore everything that is Western, to worship the foreign civilization simply because it is foreign, powerful and materially imposing. This 'Westernization' is the strongest reason why the Traditions of our Prophet and, along with them, the whole structure of the Sunnah have become so unpopular today. The Sunnah is so obviously opposed to the fundamental ideas

underlying Western civilization that those who are fascinated by the latter see no way out of the tangle but to describe the Sunnah as an irrelevant, and therefore not compulsory, aspect of Islam – because it is 'based on unreliable Traditions'. After that, it becomes easier to twist the teachings of the Qur'an in such a way that they might appear to suit the spirit of Western civilization.[31]

Bound to Fail

Those who try to deprive the Muslim community of this great source of life, guidance and strength, raising doubts about the Ḥadīth and its value as a source of legislation do not seem to realize the extent of the harm they are causing. They cannot be aware that their attempts deprive their Muslim community of its great legacy, leaving it without roots, lost, miserable. They stand in the same position towards their Muslim community as the enemies of Christianity and Judaism adopt towards these two religions. Should they be doing this, aware of its sig-nificance, then they would be the worst enemies of Islam and the Muslim community. Without the Ḥadīth and the Sunnah, there is no way to regenerate the Islamic sense and temperament which characterized the Prophet's com-panions. Such sense and temperament can only be brought about through direct companionship with the Prophet or through the *aḥādīth* which represent a perfect model of the first Islamic community and a vivid picture showing all the distinctive characteristics of the social set up established

[31] Muhammad Asad, *Islam at the Crossroads*, Dar al-Andalus Ltd, Gibraltar, 1982, pp. 92-3.

by the Prophet ﷺ. Muhammad Asad correctly describes such hostility to Islam as a conspiracy aiming to deprive the Muslim community of its indispensable source of strength:

> The Sunnah is the iron framework of the House of Islam; and if you remove the framework of a building, can you be surprised if it breaks down like a house of cards?[32]

Asad also draws attention to the inevitable consequences of denying the authority of *aḥādīth* and decrying the need to follow the Prophet in all aspects of life:

> In this way [i.e. by rejecting the Sunnah and denying the duty to follow it] the exceptional position of Islam as a moral and practical, individual and social code would be utterly destroyed.[33]

Attempts to cast doubt on the authority and authenticity of Ḥadīth as well as calls to reject the Sunnah altogether have been mooted at different levels. Different religious, political and personal motives encouraged such calls and attempts at different times. Some people may support such efforts in order to justify their negligence of Islamic duties. Yet despite all such efforts, the Sunnah maintained its place at the heart of the Islamic faith. Indeed it goes deep into the very fabric of every Muslim community and mixes with its soul. Indeed it is practically impossible to separate it from any Muslim community worthy of the name, or to establish a new Muslim community based on the Qur'an only, to the exclusion of the Sunnah. Indeed, implemen-

---

32 Asad, ibid, p. 82.

33 Asad, ibid, p. 92.

tation of the Qur'an relies to a great extent on the practical example set by the Prophet, his explanations of the Qur'an and his outlining the details of what the Qur'an states in general terms.

وَأَنزَلْنَآ إِلَيْكَ ٱلذِّكْرَ لِتُبَيِّنَ لِلنَّاسِ مَا نُزِّلَ إِلَيْهِمْ وَلَعَلَّهُمْ يَتَفَكَّرُونَ ﴿٤٤﴾

> "*We have now bestowed on you the Reminder that you may elucidate to mankind all that has been bestowed on them from on high.*" [Al-Naḥl 16: 44].

The Ḥadīth continues to enjoy in-depth scholarly attention, with its treasures being thoroughly checked and old manuscripts being published. It provides the guiding light with which to judge social norms and practices in the Muslim community. It motivates Muslims to attend to their duty of enjoining right and preventing wrong, refuting deviation in religious matters and rejecting the blind imitation of the values and practices of Western civilization. Indeed it is only through the Sunnah that the Muslim community can preserve its identity. It can resist being intellectually and culturally swallowed up by the Western way of life. It can refuse to adopt such a way of life in totality without examining its details and rejecting its elements that are contrary to Islamic values. This may be cited as confirmation of the following two *aḥādīth*:

> "A group of my community will continue to ever advocate God's message, undisturbed by those who oppose them." [Related by Ibn Majah].

> "A group of my community will remain in support of the truth until the Day of Judgement." [Related by al-Ḥākim].

Those who continue to cast doubt on the authority of the Ḥadīth and reject the Sunnah fit the image drawn by an old Arab poet, in which a deer tries to remove a solid rock by repeatedly hitting it with his horns. The rock remains solidly in place, but all that the deer achieves is to injure himself.

BIBLIOGRAPHY

Asad, Muhammad: *Islam at the Crossroads*, (Dar al-Andalus Ltd, Gibraltar, 1982).

al-Aṣbahānī, Abū Nuʿaym: *Tārīkh Aṣbahān*.

Azami, M. M.: *Studies in Hadith Methodology and Literature*, (American Trust Publication, Indianapolis, 1977)

——: *Studies in Early Hadith Literature*, (the same publisher, 1978).

al-ʿAẓīmābādī, Shams al-Haq: *ʿAwn al-Maʿbūd* (commentaries on Abū Dāwūd's *Sunan*).

al-Bukhārī, Imam: *Al-Jamiʿ al-Ṣaḥīḥ*.

al-Dehlawi, Shah Waliyullah: *Ḥujjat Allah al-Bālighah*, Vol. 1, p. 106.

al-Dhahbī, Imam Shamsuddin Muhammad (d. 748): *Tadhkirat al-Ḥuffāẓ*.

Encyclopaedia Britannica: 14th edition, Vol. XIII, pp. 16-17.

Ibn Anas, Imam Mālik: *al-Muwaṭṭa'*.

Ibn ʿAbd al-Barr, Abū ʿUmar Yūsuf b. Abdullah: *Jāmiʿ Bayān al-ʿIlm*. Vol.1 p. 76.

Ibn ʿAbd al-Ḥakam: *Sīrat ʿUmar ibn ʿAbd al-ʿAzīz*, p. 167.

Ibn Munabbih, Hammām: *Ṣaḥīfah*.

Ibn al-Ṣalāḥ, Imam Abu ʿAmr: *ʿUlūm al-Ḥadīth,* pp. 14-15.

Jewish Encyclopaedia: (Vol. 11 p. 569 & Vol. 12, p. 690).

Muslim, Imam: *Al-Jamiʿ al-Ṣaḥīḥ*.

al-Luckhnawī, ʿAbd al-Ḥayy ibn ʿAbd al-Ḥalīm (d. 1304 AH): *Al-Taʿlīq al-Mumajjad ʿalā Muwaṭṭa' Muhammad*.

Nadwi, Syed Sulaiman: *Muhammad: the Ideal Prophet*, (Arabic ed. p98).

al-Qasṭalānī, Imam Shihabuddin: *Irshād al-Sārī*.

Schweitzer, Albert: *The Quest of Historical Jesus*.

al-Sibāʿī, Muṣṭafā: *Al-Sunnah wa Makānatuhā fi al-Tashrīʿ al-Islamī*, (Damascus, pp. 58-66).

Sirhindi, Shaikh Ahmad: *Mukatabat Imam Rabbani*, Vol. II, Letter No. 100.

al-Tirmidhī, Imam: *al-ʿIlal*.